Activating the Promises of God through Prayer

By

Debby Gautreaux

Published by:

McDougal & Associates
18896 Greenwell Springs Road
Greenwell Springs, LA 70739
www.thepublishedword.com

McDougal & Associates is an organization dedicated to the spreading the Gospel of the Lord Jesus Christ to as many people as possible in the shortest time possible.

ISBN: 978-1-940461-21-2

Printed on demand in the U.S., the U.K. and Australia
For Worldwide Distribution

Dedication

I dedicate this book:

To my husband, **Russell Gautreaux**, PhD

To my children, **Jennifer Lynne Forsey** and **Jeffrey Robillard**.

To the memory of my dad, **Debbie Lee George:**
For all the times you supported me with strength and love. You were an incredible man who provided for his family and made sure that his children had the guidance they needed. I am grateful for the wisdom you gave me through the years. Thank you for long talks and always being willing to listen. You taught me how to ride a horse, change the oil in my car, pay bills, and run your business. I will miss you every day.

I remember one story in particular: the day I graduated from high school you bought me a car. I hadn't expected it. You told me to walk down the street to the gas station and pick up my car. You had the station attendant put new tires on it and fill it with gas, the insurance was paid, and I could just drive it right out of there.

I remember pulling out of the gas station that day, thinking how proud you were of me. I called you later that day to thank you, and you told me, "I am proud of you." I always said I loved you before hanging up the phone. You were such a good dad! Thanks for all things you did for me. You asked me to write a book, so I did, and now I dedicate this book to you the BEST DAD ever!

Your Daughter, Debby

Acknowledgments

I would like to thank the **Holy Spirit** for His guidance in helping me to write this book. I could not have done it on my own.

Contents

Holy Spirit, thank You.

We welcome You now.

We invite You to help us and guide us in this, our time of prayer.

God has now revealed to us his mysterious will regarding Christ
—which is to fulfill his own good plan.
Ephesians 1:9, NLT

Introduction

At the age of three, I was placed in a Catholic orphanage where I stayed until I was ten. I was put there, along with my other siblings, because my mother and father were having a custody battle at the time. Life in the orphanage wasn't easy at all, and I missed my parents every single day.

I never really understood what happened. My mother had told me that I was to stay in the orphanage until the two of them had worked out their custody arrangements, but when I was ten, it was my father who came and took me out of the orphanage, and I began a new life. It felt good to leave the orphanage, but always felt rejected by my parents.

At the age of eighteen, I married and quickly had two children. When that marriage ended, I began a downhill journey into drugs. My life had always been full of addictions. Both of my parents and also my ex-husband were addicted to drugs and alcohol, and so life had never been easy. Now addiction took me in its grip too. But, thank God, He saved me, and I was eventually able to marry again.

Sadly, that marriage, too, was full of drugs at the beginning, but then God set me free through His Holy Spirit. I had been oppressed by demonic influences, but God set me free from them, and I give Him all the glory!

I am now in my third marriage, this time to Russell Gautreaux, a minister of the Gospel, and he has given me love, support and security. Together we established Fire House Ministry, an outreach ministry that helps those in need. I am so thankful for my life now, totally and completely free from addictions. It has been so good to know that God can and will peel back every hurt and infuse us with His love.

My mission now is to help others, through prayer, and activate the blessings of God in their lives. It can be done with the Lord's guidance and complete surrender, along with repentance. My hope is for all believers to come to a place in life where there is full assurance of who they are in Christ and discover what God has for them.

I pray that you will be blessed by reading this book. Pick it up every day during your daily prayer time and let the Holy Spirit guide you, speak to you and change you into His image.

Debby Gautreaux
Baton Rouge, Louisiana

Part I

The Various Types of Prayer

Prayers of Intercession

But when you pray, go to your room, close the door and pray to your Father, who is unseen. And your Father, who sees what you do in private, will reward you.

Some translations say, *"will openly reward you."* There is a reward for prayer.

Let's begin by defining the word *intercession*. Intercession is "the action of intervening on behalf of another." Notice, that it calls this an action. We all know what an action word is, but many times when we think about prayer, we want to pray, but we often don't do it, because there is no action. Prayer requires action. Common things that keep me from prayer are being worried, tired or just busy. If I can just quiet my heart and focus on the one I know is waiting for me, then I can enter into prayer.

Prayer is a very powerful and effective tool given to us by the Holy Spirit, for it is God's way of initiating true communication with His children. If you have accepted Jesus Christ into your heart, then you are in a true relationship with God. Through that relationship, communication is accomplished through prayer. In that communication, we learn a lot of who we are as children of God, what our position is and who God is. In order for us to learn anything at all, we must also allow Him to speak back to us. This can take some special action on our part. We may have to sit for a while and just listen.

The best place to commune with God is different for everyone. It should be a place where you can be quiet before Him, so that He can begin to speak. One of my favorite spots for God to speak to me is in our backyard. Often, I will just sit there in my chair, waiting for God to speak to me. I bring my Bible out to my chair and start reading it out loud. I pray before I read, and usually the Lord will have a certain scripture pop out at me. Sometimes I go into a closet and just wait there. Wherever I pray, I can lay all of my burdens down, telling my Lord everything. I trust that through this book God will speak to you; peace will come on you like a blanket, and you will experience His glory. His Word declares:

Psalm 34:18, YLT
> *Near is Jehovah to the broken of heart,*
> *And the bruised of spirit He saveth.*

There can be many ways to enter into our "prayer closet," but there is only one true God, and we can only come to the Father through His Son, Jesus Christ. There is an order and a plan that He has put into place so that we can meet with Him on a regular basis.

My husband often comments that I am a gifted intercessor, and, yes, there are times when God gives me seasons to pray for special needs. But I also believe that we can all pray, and we all *should* pray. At times God's grace will come upon my life to pray for a certain situation, and then I believe the gift my husband is talking about begins to manifest itself. I wouldn't want anyone to think; however, that God has given me something they cannot possess. That's just not sound doctrine. I do believe that God gives special anointings to each of us according to our office. Later in the book, I will explain this more in detail.

God said:

2 Chronicles 7:14
> *If my people, who are called by my name, will humble themselves and pray and seek*
> *my face and turn from their wicked ways, then I will hear from heaven and will forgive*
> *their sin and will heal their land.*

But do you want to humble yourself to pray? As I said, there are gifts that God gives us as individuals, but we *all* can pray. I think we just need to take the time to do it.

Prayers of Thanksgiving
(Giving God All the Glory)

Enter into His gates with thanksgiving,
And into His courts with praise.
Be thankful to Him, and bless His name.   Psalm 100:4, NKJV

After we have closed the door and started to pray to our Father, the first important thing to do is to give Him praises (admiration) or thanksgiving. The prayer of thanksgiving is one of the most powerful, and it is one of my favorites. When we start to thank God for all that He is and all that He has done, faith begins to stir in us, bringing joy to our heart. In that time of joy and thanksgiving, God is moving, adjusting, changing, shifting, while growing you up to be the child He has destined you to become.

In those moments, we can come off of spiritual milk and begin to eat the meat of God's Word. Why? Because thanksgiving means "to express gratitude," and that changes everything around you. It pushes the negative out of your mind, causing your focus to shift away from your problems and onto the Lord. And it is in that atmosphere that your relationship with Him can grow by leaps and bounds.

As your relationship with the Lord grows, through prayers of thanksgiving and the atmosphere of love they create, that you begin to trust Him more, believe in His power and, consequently, begin laying all at His feet. What joy it is to know that you have the King of Kings on your side, that He loves everything about you and is concerned about every detail of your life.

God's Word says in Philippians 4:6-7, NKJV:

Be anxious [experiencing worry, unease, or nervousness, typically about an imminent event or something with an uncertain outcome] *for nothing, but in everything by prayer and supplication, with thanksgiving* [expressed gratitude], *let your requests be made known to God; and the peace of God, which surpasses all understanding, will guard your hearts and minds through Christ Jesus.*

Notice that it tells us not be worried about or nervous about an event that may or may not even occur. You may be unsure of how a certain bill will be paid, the outcome of a pending court decision or even how your child will be set free from drugs. All these events cause us to become nervous and uneasy, but we must bring everything to the Lord in prayer and thank Him for His power to change every situation. Thank Him for who He is and all that He has done and will do for you.

Right now, I encourage you stop what you are doing and start to thank God. Once a thankful spirit is created around you, you will begin to experience a joyful noise beginning to stir in your belly.

Psalm 100:1-5, ESV
(A Psalm for giving thanks)

Make a joyful noise to the LORD, all the earth!
  Serve the LORD with gladness!
  Come into his presence with singing!
Know that the LORD, he is God!
  It is he who made us, and we are his;
  We are his people, and the sheep of his pasture.
Enter his gates with thanksgiving,
  and his courts with praise!
  Give thanks to him; bless his name!
For the LORD is good;
  his steadfast love endures forever,
  and his faithfulness to all generations.

Isn't it good to know that when we give God a thankful heart, we are refreshed and encouraged in our spirit? No more discouragement and no more depression is present.

We shake off that old wine skin, as He gives us a new one. Seemingly, you will find all of your troubles fading away when you come into His presence with a thankful heart.

For this reason, 1 Thessalonians 5:18 (ESV) encourages us:

Give thanks in all circumstances; for this is the will of God in Christ Jesus for you.

When? In all circumstances. So, let us pray.

Father,

I thank You with a joyful noise right now. Out of my mouth, I thank You for giving me Your Word to feast upon. I thank You for giving me understanding to know Your Word. I thank You for helping me because You are the Lord of Lords and King of Kings, and through You I have a wonderful relationship in which I can express myself by making a joyful noise with uplifted hands.

As I continue to come into Your courtyard with praise of gratitude, I know that You are listening, bending Your ear down to hear my every word. Heavenly Father, thank You that our relationship is forever. Your love continues to draw me closer to Your loving arms.

Thank You, Lord,

Amen!

Prayers of a Grateful Heart

Thank You, Lord, for giving me a grateful heart.
Thank You for leading me beside still waters.

Thank You for a joyful heart, in my life, my spouse's life, my children's lives, and on my job.
Thank You for giving me healing in my mind, body and soul.

Thank You for helping me to see the truth in Your Word.
Thank You that I hear Your voice.

Thank You for opening doors that no man can shut.
Thank You for setting my husband free from this world.

Thank You for giving me favor with my landlord, my mortgage company and with bill collectors.
Thank You for allowing me to come into Your presence.

Thank You for giving me favor with my children to speak into their life.
Thank You that I am free from debt.

Thank You for helping me to stay focused on the task at hand.
Thank You for setting my children free.

Thank You for not letting my foot slip into a snare.
Thank You for setting me free.

Thank You for wisdom, understanding and boldness.
Thank You for revelation from Your Word. Let it come into my heart, breaking rebellious areas.
Thank You that I am not addicted to anything of this world—including, strife, TV and the Internet.

A Personal Exercise

Ask God to show you areas in your life in which you need to be more thankful. Then write those areas below.

A Personal Exercise

Write below some thankful expressions to God. For example: "Thank You, Lord, for helping me to pay my bills."

Prayers of Praise
(Going to a New Level)

Sing to the LORD!
  Give praise to the LORD!
He rescues the life of the needy
  from the hands of the wicked.   Jeremiah 20:13

A prayer of praise is another kind of prayer to God. *Praise* means "to express a warm approval or admiration of, commend, admiration for, applaud, or to sing the praise of." Through our praises to God, a beauty from Him comes in. The sound of music and expressions from your heart will begin to flow to Him, as you express your love for Him. And, through this, your relationship begins to grow.

You may think that your voice doesn't sound very good to God, but it does! This is a faith relationship, and God is looking at your heart. Do not worry about how well you sing. As your melody of praise is lifted to God, He can hear the beat of your heart toward Him. His Word says:

Psalm 100:2

Worship the LORD with gladness
come before him with joyful songs.

Often, I may lift my hands to the Father as if to say, "Father, lift me into Your arms like a child and carry me."

Sometimes, in praise, we also use the expression of dance to express our love to God.

19

Psalm 149:3, ESV

Let them praise his name with dancing,
 making melody to him with tambourine and lyre!

Any movement that expresses words can be called a dance. In biblical times, David actually appointed or put into place certain Levities to lead worship before the Ark of the Covenant. This was done to declare that God was a good God and to celebrate the wonderful works that He had done for the Israelites. Also, David released worship to be recorded as a reminder to the people of what God had done.

1 Chronicles 16:4

He [David] appointed [of a time or place decided on beforehand; designated] some of the Levites to minister before the Ark of the LORD, to extol, thank, and praise the LORD, the God of Israel.

During our times of despair, the best thing we can do is lift our hands to the Lord, lift our voices to Him and praise Him for what He has done for us in the past. As you remember the great things He has done for you, you may be reminded of a time He drew a loved one close to Him when it seemed that loved one would perish. You may be reminded of Him helping you to pay a bill that seemed impossible to get paid. Of course, we must always remember that He is the One who has given us life. All this can be expressed in many ways: through dance, the clapping of hands, singing, meditating, or even through acts of service.

What a beautiful thing it is when we praise God with music, when we can lift our voices in harmony with each other and give Him praise. Many times, when I praise God, a certain song will come to me, as if it is an anthem for my current situation. Recently, I went through a conflict with a sister in the Lord. I really didn't know what to do about the situation. I wasn't angry with her; I just felt uneasy when I was in her presence.

I didn't think that I should call her. I really didn't know what to do. Then, while I was praying one day, I felt in my spirit to buy her a gift. All week I prayed and one day a song came into my spirit, "If I give all to You, You will make all things new." I began to sing this song over and over in my heart. I would pray, "I am giving this person to You, Lord. Help me to work this situation out." That night when I saw her at a service, I walked up to her, gave her the gift and hugged her. In that moment, I knew in my heart that it was a done deal. Whatever had been causing the conflict between us was fixed. Why? Because a Spirit of praise came upon me, to help me and give me a breakthrough in that situation.

God is so good. I know that He destroyed that spirit of opposition, strife, and disagreement through praise that day. It all started with my heart lifting up a praise to Him. This was just like King Jehoshaphat who appointed men to sing to God during his battles.

2 Chronicles 20:20-23

Early in the morning they left for the Desert of Tekoa. As they set out, Jehoshaphat stood and said, "Listen to me, Judah and people of Jerusalem! Have faith in the Lord your God and you will be upheld; have faith in his prophets and you will be successful." After consulting the people, Jehoshaphat appointed men to sing to the Lord and to praise him for the splendor of his holiness as they went out at the head of the army, saying:

"Give thanks to the Lord,

for his love endures forever."

As they began to sing and praise, the Lord set ambushes against the men of Ammon and Moab and Mount Seir who were invading Judah, and they were defeated.

I had answered an appointment to sing to the Lord that day, and as a result, my enemy was also defeated, the enemy of unforgiveness.

Father,

I pray with uplifted hands, thanking You for defeating the enemy in my life. Although my situation may look impossible, and I don't know what to do or what to say in my conflict, help me to do my part by making peace with others that I have a disagreement with, so that I can forgive quickly. I don't want to give any foothold to the enemy. Help me to shut any and every door that I have opened through unforgiveness. Even when I feel that I did nothing wrong, please help me to love that person anyway, so I can pass this test by showing Your love through an act of kindness and by praying for this person. Give me a song that I can lift to You, so that You will move on my behalf. When the praise goes up, Your glory will come down, and Your presence will speak to me.

In Jesus' name,
Amen!

Prayers of Agreement
(Bringing Unity to Your Life)

Again, truly I tell you that if two of you on earth agree about anything they ask for, it will be done for them by my Father in heaven. For where two or three gather in my name, there am I with them. Matthew 18:19-20

While all of our individual prayers are important, many times God will send people to stand in the gap to believe with us. Agreement among two, several or more is shown in the Bible to be very important. It brings in the anointing and the presence of God. Here is that promise again:

Again, truly I tell you that if two of you on earth agree about anything they ask for, it will be done for them by my Father in heaven. For where two or three gather in my name, there am I with them. Matthew 18:19-20

As we see in this text, when we gather together, God is there standing and waiting for us to invite Him into our situation. Agreement brings His presence to us.

The next verse shows that agreement and forgiveness go hand in hand.

Then Peter came to Jesus and asked, "Lord, how many times shall I forgive my brother who sins against me? Up to seven times?" Matthew 18:21

You can't have one without the other. Forgiveness is a vital part of our life, and although you may think you have every right to be bitter or angry with someone, God just does not see it that way. As you can see in this text, Peter asked Jesus how many times he should forgive his brother, and Jesus' reply was simple:

Jesus answered, "I tell you, not just seven times, but seventy-seven times!"

Matthew 18:22

Many times, I must say to myself, "I forgive "So and So" for whatever reason. Even if I don't feel it in that moment, I speak it out in faith. Then, on another day I may think of that person and realize that I feel no bitterness at all toward them. Bitterness means that you are angry or disappointed because you feel that you have been treated unfairly, so you hold a resentment against the person who did you wrong.

Each heart knows its own bitterness,
  and no one else can share its joy.

Proverbs 14:10

Dr. Dean Amish has said, "Harboring a root of bitterness can be deadly to your health. When people feel bitter they often shut others out and then loneliness and depression set in. Study after study has shown that people who feel lonely, depressed and isolated are many times more likely to get sick and die prematurely—not only of heart disease, but from virtually all causes—than those who have a sense of connection, love and community."[1]

This is the reason God has set up a plan to defeat every problem we may have. When we feel lonely or depressed, all we must do is step out in faith, call a friend and come into agreement with them in prayer for our problem. How wonderful is that? If we tap into this source God has given us called "agreement," we can get through any problem life may throw at us. Our next exercise will help you to step out of your comfort zone and into the zone of agreement.

I have noticed that very often the enemy tries to keep us from coming into agreement with another believer. He wants you to let time go by, and soon a big gap will

---

1. Dr. Dean Omish, MD, quoted on WebMD

develop between you and a family member. You and I have been given a commission from God, to have a ministry of reconciliation:

2 Corinthians 5:18-21

All of this is from God, who reconciled us to himself through Christ and gave us the ministry of reconciliation; that God was reconciling the world to himself in Christ, not counting people's sins against them. And he has committed to us the message of reconciliation. We are therefore Christ's ambassadors, as though God were making his appeal through us. We implore you on Christ's behalf: Be reconciled to God. God made him who had no sin to be sin for us, so that in him we might become the righteousness of God.

We must do everything in our power to maintain unity with others. We can do this by reconciling in the Spirit, asking God through prayer to help us to show His love and not hold on to unforgiveness or bitterness. I believe that God will surely help us to "let go and let God." On the next page is an exercise to help you pray for reconciliation between yourself and any person you may feel bitterness toward.

A Prayer Exercise

Call a friend or a loved one you harbor something against. Write below who you called and how it made you feel after you called them.

A Prayer Exercise

Look up Bible verses on joy, peace and love and write them in the space below:

A Prayer Exercise

Write down the name of anyone you may have bitterness against for any reason and, beside their name, write out a prayer of forgiveness.

An Example of a Prayer of Forgiveness

Father, I lift my heart and life to You today and I ask You to forgive me for having unforgiveness toward _____ _____. Wash me in Your blood. Help me to cast down anything in my mind that would continually replay what this person has done to me. You said in Your Word (Matthew 6:14) "For if you forgive others their trespasses, your heavenly Father will also forgive you." This means that I must forgive because I love You. So, by faith I forgive _____.

Right now, I thank You for accepting me as Your child, forgiven, set free from any attitude that is displeasing to You. Give me a heart to love this person, as You would have me to love them.

In Jesus' name I pray,
Amen!

"Man has two great spiritual needs.
One is for forgiveness.
The other is for goodness."
— Billy Graham

Another Type of Prayer for Forgiveness

There is another prayer that we can pray on the topic of unforgiveness. Insert the person's name in the blanks below.

Colossians 1:3-14

We always thank God, the Father of our Lord Jesus Christ, when we pray for [insert the person's name here] _____ because we have heard of _____'s faith in Christ Jesus and of the love _____ [has] for all God's people the faith and love that spring from the hope stored up for _____ in heaven and about which _____ [has] already heard in the true message of the gospel that has come to _____. In the same way, the gospel is bearing fruit and growing throughout the whole world just as it has been doing among _____ since the day _____ heard it and truly understood God's grace. _____ learned it from Epaphras, our dear fellow servant, who is a faithful minister of Christ on our behalf, and who also told us of _____'s love in the Spirit.

For this reason, since the day we heard about _____, we have not stopped praying for _____. We continually ask God to fill _____ with the knowledge of his will through all the wisdom and understanding that the Spirit gives, so that _____ may live a life worthy of the Lord and please him in every way: bearing fruit in every good work, growing in the knowledge of God, being strengthened with all power according to his glorious might so that _____ may have great endurance and patience, and giving joyful thanks to the Father, who has qualified _____ to share in the inheritance of his holy people in the kingdom of light. For he has rescued us from the dominion of darkness and brought us into the kingdom of the Son he loves, in whom we have redemption, the forgiveness of sins.

Prayers of Binding and Loosing
(Loose Your Breakthrough)

And I will give unto thee the keys of the kingdom of heaven: whatever you bind on earth will be bound in heaven, and whatever you loose on earth will be loosed in heaven.

Matthew 16:19

Here in Matthew, Jesus gives us an important weapon we can use against the enemy. It is called "binding and loosing." The Scriptures show that binding is like a temporary spiritual handcuffing. Binding is "the action of fastening, holding together." It means:

- to bind tie, fasten
- to bind, fasten with chains, to throw into chains
- to bind, put under obligation, of the law, duty etc.
- to forbid, prohibit, declare to be illicit

We can bind all spiritual negatives trying to influence our life. For instance, if you are having financial difficulties, you can bind anything that would hinder your finances from flowing from Heaven. In other words, we can bind lack and loose wealth from Heaven over our life.

To *loose* means "to set free; release." Loosing, like binding, can be done here on earth and takes effect in the spiritual realm. Loosing can refer to the loosing of a captive or person in bondage. You can bind demons, and you can loose captives.

31

When Jesus set the woman with the issue of blood free, He said to her, *"Woman, thou art loosed from thine infirmity"* (Luke 13:12, KJV).

It is very important in our prayer life that we take back what it rightfully ours, and we must press through every attack on our life. God is so good that He always has a plan for our life, for us to get back to the abundance that He longs for us to have. No one should go without, if you are a child of the King, and if you have asked Jesus to take control of your heart and life. Many people believe that God wants you to settle for less, but in His Word He makes clear that He wants us to move from ordinary to extraordinary. He wants us to go from being satisfied to helping others.

Many times, when we tap into the wealth of God, it is to help others and thus spread the love of God. In these acts of love, God is lifted up and glorified. Today, you can believe for the impossible and cross over the river to the abundant life that God wants you to have. Just believe, and all things can change in an instant through a prayer of binding and loosing.

I will give you an example of a prayer that will help you cross over to a life of sharing God's love with others. As your own prayers come to mind, write them down and use them as needed:

Father,

Thank You for giving us the keys to the Kingdom of Heaven, and we take You at Your Word. We bind any strife, fear, torment, sickness, opposition, lack, hindrance, or blockage in our life that concerns us and our family, especially when it comes to our finances.

Father, we loose Your freedom into our lives. We loose abundance. We loose wealth and overflow. We loose life. We loose goodness. We loose Your angels to minister abundance in our homes, so that we can help others in their time of need and, thus, show forth the love of God.

In Jesus name I pray,

Amen!

Prayers of Binding and Loosing

- I have the keys of the Kingdom. Whatever I bind on Earth is bound in Heaven, and whatever I loose on Earth is loosed in Heaven (Matthew 16:19).
- I bind the kings in chains and the nobles with fetters of iron (Psalm 149:8).
- I bind the strongman that spoils my goods (Matthew 12:29).
- I bind Leviathan and all proud spirits arrayed against my life (Job 41:5).
- I bind the principalities, powers and rulers of the darkness of this world and spiritual wickedness [evil] in high places (Ephesians 6:12).
- I bind all sickness and disease released against my mind or body.
- Let the chains be loosed around my neck, feet and back (Isaiah 51:14).
- Let the prisoners be loosed and set free (Psalm 146:7).
- Loose my neck from all bands of headaches, earaches, sore throat and coughing (Isaiah 52:2).
- I loose myself from all bands of wickedness (Isaiah 58:6).
- I loose my mind, will and emotions used by Satan to bring me into spiritual darkness, in the name of Jesus.
- I loose my city and region from every assignment of Hell, and I take back every assignment for the glory of God
- I loose my finances from every spirit of poverty, lack, and debt.
- I loose myself from all generational curses and hereditary spirits (Galatians 3:13).
- I loose myself from every assignment against me caused by a generational curse of witchcraft, sorcery or divination.
- I loose myself, my children, and other family members from the chains of addiction to drugs and smoking.
- I loose myself from any setbacks or hurt caused by others.
- I loose myself from any pain in my body.
- I loose finances in my life that are held back by generational curses.
- I loose raises and bonuses from my job and any other benefits that are being withheld.
- I loose favor around me from others to help me when I need it.
- I loose Your wisdom, knowledge and understanding to solve problems in my life
- I loose Your healing power for my family, friends and others who are in the hospital.
- I loose Your anointing on my life so that I can be of service to my church.

Prayers of Spiritual Warfare

For our struggle is not against flesh and blood [humans], but against the rulers [forces], against the authorities [government], against the powers of this dark world and against the spiritual forces of evil in the heavenly [or heaven] realms. Ephesians 6:12

Intercession can also be called "spiritual warfare," and it is the key to God's battle plan for our lives. The battlefield is not here on earth against other peolpe, but it is in the heavenliness against darkness. This war is characterized by extreme collective aggression, destruction, and usually high mortality. But it is not our side that loses, but the evil that we fight against. Thank the Lord we have the victory through Christ Jesus, but we must take our stand and fight on the wall of prayer.

Isaiah 38:2

Hezekiah turned his face to the wall and prayed to the LORD.

You and I must also turn our face to the wall and pray, because anytime we move toward God, there is a force that is trying to hinder our progress. If we try to preach the Gospel, the enemy is there to try to hinder our progress, so that the Gospel will not reach the hearts and minds of people that are hurting. Why? Because the evil forces do not want us to live a life full of freedom and liberty. Jesus clearly identified His foe and his tactics:

John 10:10, KJV

The thief cometh not, but for to steal, and to kill, and to destroy [put an end to the existence of something by damaging or attacking it]: *I am come that they might have life, and that they might have it more abundantly.*

So, if you're sick in your body, the enemy does not want you to have a life full of healing. Often we say things like "I'm hurting," "I don't feel good, "or "I am depressed." We must push back against the spiritual force that tell us these things. Our enemy is constantly trying to put an end to us or to damage our life. His is an evil attack. But God has a great plan to help us in these situations. It is called "the Armor of God" (see the graphic on the next page). As with prayer, we cannot think this armor into place. We must make a concerted action to see that we are well protected.

Putting on the Whole Armor of God

Say this aloud:

Father God,

I put on every piece of the armor You have provided, so that I will be able to resist every attack of the enemy. Then, after the battle is finished, I will still be standing firm. I will stand my ground, by putting on the belt of truth and the body armor of Your righteousness. I put my shoes on, so that I will have the peace that comes from the Good News. I will be fully prepared. In addition to these, I hold up the shield of faith to stop the fiery arrows of the devil. I put on salvation as my helmet, protecting my mind, and I take the sword of the Spirit, which is Your Word.

Amen!

Ephesians 6:11-18
Put on the full armor of God, so that you can take your stand against the devil's schemes. For our struggle is not against flesh and blood, but against the rulers, against the authorities, against the powers of this dark world and against the spiritual forces of evil in the heavenly realms. Therefore put on the full armor of God, so that when the day of evil comes, you may be able to stand your ground, and after you have done everything,

The Armor of God

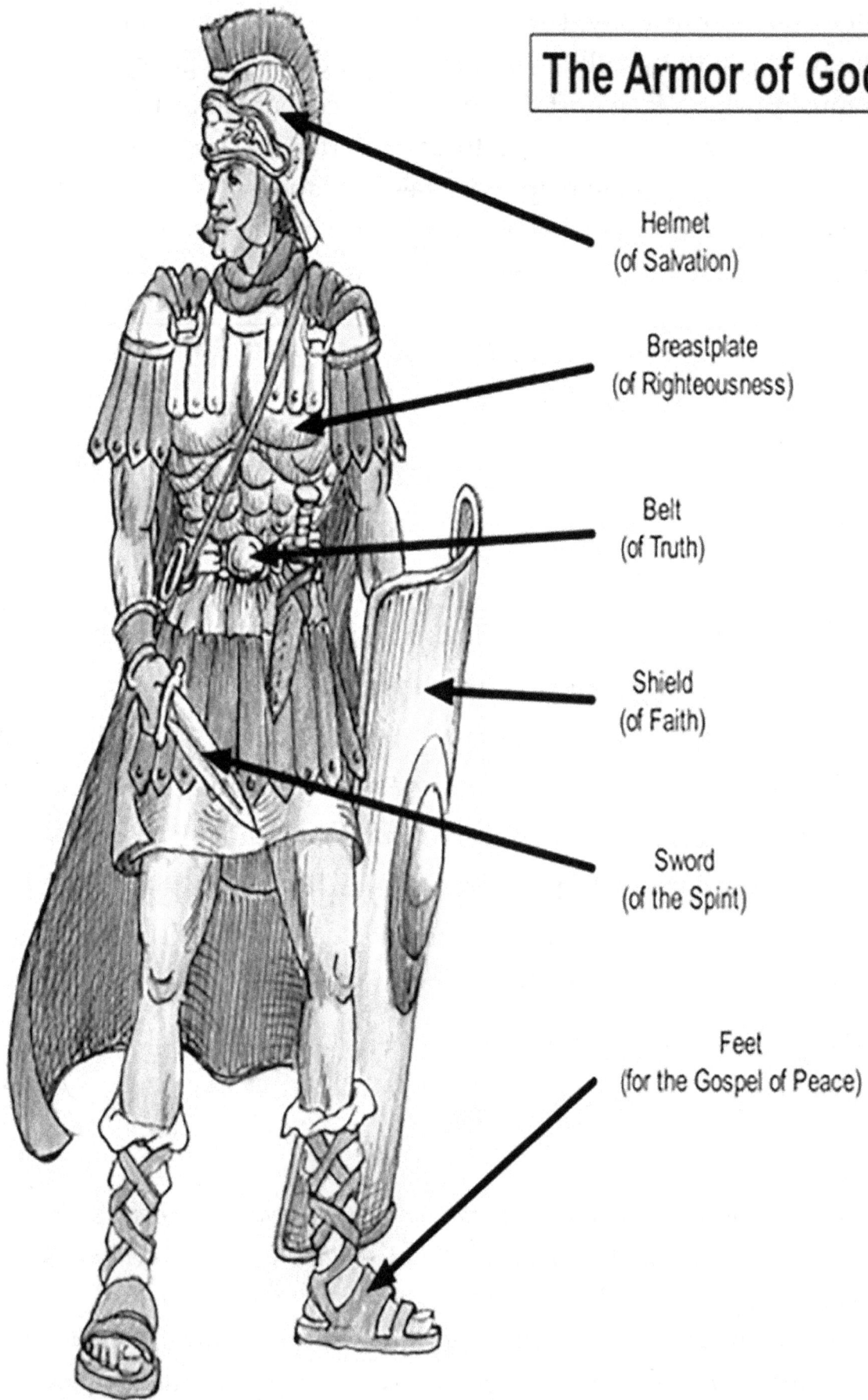

Helmet
(of Salvation)

Breastplate
(of Righteousness)

Belt
(of Truth)

Shield
(of Faith)

Sword
(of the Spirit)

Feet
(for the Gospel of Peace)

to stand. Stand firm then, with the belt of truth buckled around your waist, with the breastplate of righteousness in place, and with your feet fitted with the readiness that comes from the gospel of peace. In addition to all this, take up the shield of faith, with which you can extinguish all the flaming arrows of the evil one. Take the helmet of salvation and the sword of the Spirit, which is the word of God. And pray in the Spirit on all occasions with all kinds of prayers and requests. With this in mind, be alert and always keep on praying for all the Lord's people.

Notice again the action words used here. We must act by declaring today I **put on** the helmet of salvation, the belt of truth and the shoes of peace. I **hold up** my shield of faith and **take up** the sword of the Spirit. Just as in war, when soldiers dig a trench, a long, narrow ditch, I must leave no opening for the enemy to come in. Today I act in faith and close all entrances that surround me.

How do we do this, my friend? We do it in prayer. This passage declares that we must pray in the Spirit always and on every occasion. So, stay alert, be persistent, and you will be victorious!

Matthew Henry's Commentary describes the various parts of the armor of God as "being for heavily-armed soldiers, those who must resist the fiercest assaults of the enemy. Notice that there is no piece of armor for the back. There is nothing to defend those who turn back from their Christian warfare.

"What is the girdle? It is truth or sincerity. This piece girds together all of the other pieces of our armor, and therefore may be the most important.

"The righteousness of Christ, imputed to us, is a breastplate against the arrows of Satan's wrath. The righteousness of Christ implanted in us fortifies the heart against his attacks.

Resolution must be our greaves, the armor for our legs, so that we can stand our ground. Our feet must be shod with the preparation of the Gospel of peace so that we can march forward in rugged terrain. Our obedience in the midst of trials must come from a clear knowledge of the Gospel.

"Faith is all in all in an hour of temptation. Faith, as relying on unseen objects, receiving Christ and the benefits of redemption, and so deriving grace from Him, is like a shield, a defense every way.

The devil is the wicked one. Violent temptations, by which the soul is set on fire of Hell, are darts Satan shoots at us. Also, hard thoughts about God and about ourselves. Faith, applying the Word of God and the grace of Christ quenches the darts of temptation.

"Salvation must be our helmet. A good hope of salvation, a scriptural expectation of victory, will purify the soul and keep it from being defiled by Satan.

"To the Christian armed for defense in battle, the apostle recommends only one weapon of attack, but it is enough. It is none other than the sword of the Spirit, which is the Word of God. It subdues and mortifies evil desires and blasphemous thoughts as they rise within and answers unbelief and error as they assault us from without. A single text, well understood, and rightly applied, at once destroys a temptation or an objection, and subdues the most formidable adversary.

"Prayer must fasten together all the other parts of our Christian armor. There are other duties of religion and of our stations in the world, but we must keep up times of prayer. We must use holy thoughts in our ordinary course. A vain heart will be vain in prayer. We must pray with all kinds of prayer (public, private, and secret; social and solitary; solemn and sudden) and with all the parts of prayer (confession of sin, petition for mercy, and thanksgiving for favors received). And we must do it by the grace of God the Holy Spirit, in dependence on, and according to, His teaching. We must preserve requests, despite discouragements. We must pray, not for ourselves only, but for all saints. Our enemies are mighty, and we are without strength, but our Redeemer is almighty, and in the power of his mighty we may overcome.

"Almighty God (El-Shaddai) is the next great title by which God reveals himself to Abraham. The term appears as 'El Shaddai' (Almighty God) seven times, and standing alone as 'Shaddai' (the Almighty) 41 times in the Old Testament and 9 times in the New Testament. An even more common title for God in the Old Testament is as 'The LORD of hosts' (Yahweh-Sabaoth), which appears nearly 250 times.

"We must remember there are more for us than against. And God has His host ready and standing on guard to protect His children. All we have to do is command His Word to go forth, and the angels will heed that Word, doing battle for us. If we know someone who does not know the truth about God, we can ask God to send His warring angels to put the armor of truth around this person so he can come to know God and have revelation to set this person free."[2]

---

2. Matthew Henry, *Matthew Henry's Concise Commentary of the Whole Bible*, Woodstock, Ontario, Canada, Devoted Publishing: 2017

A Prayer Exercise

List the various pieces of the armor of God and tell what each piece means to you. For example: The Belt of Truth—I am God's child (see John 1:12), so I come against every lie.

Part II

How to Pray Effectively

The Armor of God and Prayer

I cannot tell you how many times, when I was going through some sort of battle, God would tell me I was missing a piece of the armor for that day. This would come down as revelation so easily and hit my spirit. For instance, I would be going to prayer and think about a certain situation and how I should have handled it better, and the Holy Spirit would tell me, "You were missing a piece of armor in that situation."

Would I have the belt of truth around my waist for that day? Did I seek God and know the truth about this or that? Did I just react to something because it felt good, or it seemed I should have done it that way, because I had done it that way before? Not all situations call for the same reaction. Not all things should be handled in the same way. I tell you now, if you want to go through a battle with success, PUT ON YOUR ARMOR. We cannot assume for a moment that we do not need this armor because we do!

My husband tells those who attend his counseling seminars that the reason many people do not get healed or have some breakthrough in their inner emotions may be because they are lazy, too lazy to think the right thoughts and correct the situation. Yes, it takes a little effort on our part to do the right thing.

The armor of God is not just for defense. It is an offensive gear that we must put on to prepare for any battle. Would a football player go onto the field without his helmet on? Certainly not. That would only mean that he was risking severe head injury. And just as with football, God wants us to "gear up" every day so that we can win the "game of life." This is not meant to make us fearful, just to help us be ready for whatever comes.

If Sister "So and So" came up to you and told you that Brother So and So was having an affair, how would you react? Would you be sure to have on the belt of truth and ask God to help you remember the warnings of the Scriptures when conversations like that take place? Or would you just say, "Oh my, how terrible!" and fall right in with the gossip? Let's be aware that our reaction to things that happen around us may try to pull us out of what God wants us to do.

Say the declarations that follow on this page and the next two pages out loud. God's Word works through our spirit, and it is a spiritual cure, but, like anything else, it must be applied. God's Word can be received in your spirit, but once received there, it must thoroughly permeate the mind, will and body. God's said:

My son, pay attention to what I say;
turn your ear to my words.
Do not let them out of your sight,
keep them within your heart;
for they are life to those who find them
and health to one's whole body.
Proverbs 4:20-22

Here are the declarations:

- I am complete in Him Who is the Head of all principality and power (Colossians 2:10).
- I am alive with Christ (Ephesians 2:5).
- I am free from the law of sin and death (Romans 8:2).
- I am far from oppression, and fear does not come near me (Isaiah 54:14).
- I am born of God, and the evil one does not touch me (1 John 5:18).
- I am holy and without blame before Him in love (Ephesians 1:4 and 1 Peter 1:16).
- I have the mind of Christ (1 Corinthians 2:16 and Philippians 2:5).

Speak the following declarations over your mind. Lay your hands on your own head and speak these words over yourself:

- I have the peace of God that passes all understanding (Philippians 4:7).

- I have the Greater One living in me. Greater is He Who is in me than he who is in the world (1 John 4:4).

Say the following declarations every day, stirring up the gift of God in you. Lay your hands on your belly and say the following:

- I have received the gift of righteousness and reign as a king in life by Jesus Christ (Romans 5:17).
- I have received the Spirit of wisdom and revelation in the knowledge of Jesus, the eyes of my understanding being enlightened (Ephesians 1:17-18).
- I have received the power of the Holy Spirit to lay hands on the sick and see them recover, to cast out demons and to speak with new tongues (Mark 3:15).
- I have power over all the power of the enemy, and nothing shall by any means harm me (Mark 16:17-18 and Luke 10:17-19).
- I have put off the old man and have put on the new man, which is renewed in the knowledge after the image of Him Who created me (Colossians 3:9-10).
- I have given [and therefore God is giving back to me]. Good measure, pressed down, shaken together, and running over men give into my bosom (Luke 6:38).
- I have no lack, for my God supplies all my need according to His riches in glory by Christ Jesus (Philippians 4:19).
- I can quench all the fiery darts of the wicked one with my shield of faith (Ephesians 6:16).
- I can do all things through Christ (Philippians 4:13).
- I show forth the praises of God Who has called me out of darkness into His marvelous light (1 Peter 2:9).
- I am God's child, for I am born again of the incorruptible seed of the Word of God, which lives and abides forever (1 Peter 1:23).
- I am God's workmanship, created in Christ Jesus unto good works (Ephesians 2:10).
- I am a new creature in Christ (2 Corinthians 5:17).
- I am a spirit being alive to God (Romans 6:11 and 1 Thessalonians 5:23).
- I am a believer, and the light of the Gospel shines in my mind (2 Corinthians 4:4).
- I am a doer of the Word and blessed in my actions (James 1:22 and 25).
- I am a joint-heir with Christ (Romans 8:17).
- I am more than a conqueror through Him Who loves me (Romans 8:37).

- I am an overcomer by the blood of the Lamb and the word of my testimony (Revelation 12:11).
- I am a partaker of Christ's divine nature (2 Peter 1:3-4).
- I am an ambassador for Christ (2 Corinthians 5:20).
- I am part of a chosen generation, a royal priesthood, a holy nation, a purchased people (1 Peter 2:9).
- I am the righteousness of God in Jesus Christ (2 Corinthians 5:21).
- I am the temple of the Holy Spirit; I am not my own (1 Corinthians 6:19).
- I am the head and not the tail; I am above only and not beneath (Deuteronomy 28:13).
- I am the light of the world (Matthew 5:14).
- I am God's elect, full of mercy, kindness, humility, and longsuffering (Romans 8:33 and Colossians 3:12).
- I am forgiven of all my sins and washed in the blood of Jesus (Ephesians 1:7).
- I am delivered from the power of darkness and translated into God's Kingdom (Colossians 1:13).
- I am redeemed from the curse of sin, sickness, and poverty (Deuteronomy 28:15-68 and Galatians 3:13).
- I am firmly rooted, built up, established in my faith and overflowing with gratitude (Colossians 2:7).
- I am called of God to be the voice of His praise (Psalm 66:8 and 2 Timothy 1:9).
- I am healed by the stripes of Jesus (Isaiah 53:5 and 1 Peter 2:24).
- I am raised up with Christ and seated in heavenly places (Ephesians 2:6 and Colossians 2:12).
- I am greatly loved by God (Romans 1:7, Ephesians 2:4, Colossians 3:12 and 1 Thessalonians 1:4).
- I am strengthened with all might according to His glorious power (Colossians 1:11).
- I am submitted to God, and the devil flees from me because I resist him in the name of Jesus (James 4:7).
- I press on toward the goal to win the prize to which God in Christ Jesus is calling us upward (Philippians 3:14).
- For God has not given me a spirit of fear, but of power, love, and a sound mind (2 Timothy 1:7).

- It is not I who live, but Christ lives in me (Galatians 2:20).
- Out of my innermost being will flow rivers of living water (John 7:38).
- I am the Bride of Christ (John 3:29).
- The love of God has been poured out in my heart through Jesus' death (Romans 5:5).
- I am healed (1 Peter 2:24).
- I am sanctified by God's Spirit (John 17:17).
- I am holy and blameless (Ephesians 4:22).
- I am raised from the dead along with Christ, and I sit in heavenly places (Ephesians 2:6).
- I am God's masterpiece (Ephesians 2:10).
- I am united with Christ (Ephesians 2:13).
- I am a member of God's family (Ephesians 2:19).
- I am called to a glorious future (Ephesians 4:4).
- I have been given special gifts to be used for the Body of Christ (Ephesians 4:7).
- I have a new nature in Christ (Ephesians 4:24).
- I am blessed with every spiritual blessing (Ephesians 1:3).
- I am the light of the Lord (Ephesians 5:8).
- I am God's child (Ephesians 5:1).
- God has rescued me with His mighty power (Psalm 17:7).
- He took our sicknesses and removed them (Matthew 8:17).
- He removed the heavy yoke of oppression (Isiah 58:9).

There are many other promises in God's Word that we can claim, using them as our sword to defeat the enemy:

2 Peter 1:4

Through these he has given us his very great and precious promises, so that through them you may participate in the divine nature, having escaped the corruption in the world caused by evil desires.

A Spiritual Exercise

Find some other promises in the Bible and write them below:

Faith

Now faith is confidence is what we hope for
and assurance about what we do not see.
Hebrews 11:1

Father,

Thank You for the faith that we need for today. Father, I know that doubt may creep into my life. So, right now, I pray that You would help me to have faith to move the mountains in my life, to stand on Your promises and believe for the impossible.

Sometimes I struggle to have faith, so I ask You now for faith to move these mountains. I know that without faith I cannot please You, and my heart's desire is to have this kind of faith. I need You to come in and give me the strength and guidance that I desperately need.

Life can pull me this way and that, and I get caught up in the hustle and bustle of my circumstances. Help me to take a deep breath, slow down and just be in Your presence. I know that if I come to You and rest in Your presence, I will begin to read Your Word, and then the faith I need will begin to build in my life. Thank You for coming to me. Even when I don't feel You, I know that You are there.

In Jesus name,
Amen!

Spiritual Authority and Prayer

I have given you authority to trample on snakes and scorpions and to overcome all the power of the enemy; nothing will harm you.   Luke 10:19

Walking in authority and knowing your position in Christ is important—if you want to succeed in prayer. We cannot allow the devil to continually walk over us and steal from us. We must take our rightful position. You need the power of God to back up the Word, so you can use it in your prayer life. You need to learn to use the Word as a sword to take authority over every enemy so that you can claim what is rightfully yours as a child of God.

My life verse is Acts 1:8. It says:

But you shall receive power when the Holy Spirit comes upon you, and you shall be My witnesses in Jerusalem, in all Judea and Samaria, and to the ends of the earth. (MEV)

Every time I read this verse, the word *power* jumps out at me. As I've studied this verse of scripture, I've developed a sense of awe. The Greek word for *power* is *dunamis*, which the *Analytical Lexicon of the Greek New Testament* defines, with reference to Acts 1:8, as "able to produce a strong effect power, might, strength" and as "supernatural manifestations of power, miracles, wonders, powerful deeds." This word is used ten times in the Acts of the Apostles and is always about God's power, miracles and signs and wonders. When the Bible uses the word *dunamis*, it never refers to our own strength or ability, but rather to God's power working through us. It is His power alone that keeps us, and walking in His power and glory forms our character. This, then, is our authority.

Jesus promised His disciples:

Luke 24:49

I am going to send you what my Father has promised; but stay in the city until you have been clothed with power from on high.

Henry Thayer has written, "After the apostles were baptized with the Spirit on the Day of Pentecost, Peter and John were on their way to the Temple to pray and came across a man crippled from birth, begging. In Acts 3:6, Peter said, *'I have no silver or gold, but I give you what I have. In the name of Jesus Christ of Nazareth, rise up and walk!'* The man was healed, and Peter attributed the power displayed in Acts 3:11-16 not to himself, but to Jesus! The authorities arrested Peter and John. When they questioned the apostles, the two Christian followers said the man was healed *'by the name of Jesus Christ of Nazareth, whom you cruci-fied, and whom God raised from the dead. ... There is no salvation in any other, for there is no other name under heaven given among men by which we must be saved'* (Acts 4:8-22)."

"Authority in God's Word is a simple thing, and as we meditate on the Scriptures, we must change our viewpoint to adjust to His Word. God wants to change our viewpoint to His viewpoint.

Colossians 3:1-4

Living as Those Made Alive in Christ

Since, then, you have been raised with Christ, set your hearts on things above, where Christ is, seated at the right hand of God. Set your minds on things above, not on earth-ly things. For you died, and your life is now hidden with Christ in God. When Christ, who is your life, appears, then you also will appear with him in glory.

"We are to set our hearts on things above, where Christ is seated. We tend to view our sit-uation from our position here on the earth, but God wants our view to change. Why? Because we are now seated with Him in heavenly places, and we, therefore, have a unique authority.

"The phrase *'the right hand of God'* usually refers to strength. You've probably heard the phrase 'he's my right-hand man,' but where does this phrase come from?

I believe it comes from the Bible. This phrase 'right hand' occurs one hundred and sixty-six times in the Bible, so it is no accident and the words 'right hand' have significant meaning. God inspired Isaiah to write:

For I, the LORD your God,
*   who takes hold of your right hand*
and says to you, Do not fear;
*   I will help you.*   Isaiah 41:13

"The right hand signifies strength, perhaps because most people are right-handed, and therefore that is the hand that normally has the greatest strength. Most people write with their right hand and do difficult things with their right hand, so it is the hand where strength typically abides.

"The religious leaders were constantly trying to trap and trick Jesus with enigmatic questions. He once answered them:

The Lord said to my Lord:
*   "Sit at my right hand,*
until I make your enemies
*   a footstool for your feet."*   Luke 20:42-43

"Being at the right hand of someone who sits on a throne signifies having a place of authority. In this case, it was Jesus who sat (and still sits) at the Father's right hand. Jesus referred to this during His illegal trial by saying:

But from now on, the Son of Man will be seated at the right hand of the mighty God.
                                                                    Luke 22:69

"This is also mentioned in Mark 16, where Jesus ascended back to the Father:

So then after the Lord had spoken unto them, he was received up into heaven, and sat
on the right hand of God.   Mark 16:19, KJV

"We can see clearly that the right hand is symbolic of rulership, authority, sovereignty, blessing and strength and is significant in the Scriptures. We even see this in the separation of the sheep and goats at the judgment.

Jesus said:

All the nations will be gathered before him, and he will separate the people one from another as a shepherd separates the sheep from the goats. He will put the sheep on his right and the goats on his left.   Matthew 25:32-33

"Being on the right side is critical to our eternal destiny and fatal to those on the left. All who trust in Christ will be placed on His right side of Christ because they will have imputed to them the very righteousness of the Son of God (see 2 Corinthians 5:21)."[3]

God has given all authority to us, His children. What testimony do you have when it comes to using God's authority in your situation? Write it below:

---

3. Henry Thayer D.D., *Thayer's Greek-English Lexicon of the New Testement*, Corrected Edition,

Wisdom and Revelation and Prayer

I pray that the eyes of your heart may be enlightened in order that you may know the hope to which he has called you, the riches of his glorious inheritance in his holy people, and his incomparably great power for us who believe. Ephesians 1:18-19

During my studies at International Miracle Institute in Pensacola, Florida, I would often use our study time to meditate on Ephesians, and God opened my eyes to much revelation of that book. As I would read it, the words seemed to leap off of the pages, and I would pray those words over my children. This changed my life and gave me a whole new perspective on God's love. I began to truly understanding what He wants for us, His children. I read those passages at least three times in each sitting, so that the words would go deep inside of my spirit.

God's Word is so powerful that it will go from your head to your heart, penetrate your spirit and bring life to your flesh. I think one of the reasons God's children do not receive healing more frequently in their bodies is that we do not meditate enough on God's Word. We are to meditate on it day and night. If we would do that, I believe people would see more miracles of healing in their bodies.

Not only does God bring His Word to life; but He also uses the Word to wash our minds of old thought patterns. The anointing of God flows from the Word into your spirit and breaks bondages. Take a few minutes and prayerfully read more of this passage and those that follow. Then read them at least two more times today.

Ephesians 1:15-23

For this reason, ever since I heard about your faith in the Lord Jesus and your love for all God's people, I have not stopped giving thanks for you, remembering you in my prayers. I keep asking that the God of our Lord Jesus Christ, the glorious Father, may give you the Spirit of wisdom and revelation, so that you may know him better. I pray that the eyes of your heart may be enlightened in order that you may know the hope to which he has called you, the riches of his glorious inheritance in his holy people, and his incomparably great power for us who believe. That power is the same as the mighty strength he exerted when he raised Christ from the dead and seated him at his right hand in the heavenly realms, far above all rule and authority, power and dominion, and every name that is invoked, not only in the present age but also in the one to come. And God placed all things under his feet and appointed him to be head over everything for the church, which is his body, the fullness of him who fills everything in every way.

Ephesians 3: 11-19, NASB

This was in accordance with the eternal purpose which He carried out in Christ Jesus our Lord, in whom we have boldness and confident access through faith in Him. Therefore I ask you not to lose heart at my tribulations on your behalf, for they are your glory. For this reason I bow my knees before the Father, from whom every family in heaven and on earth derives its name, that He would grant you, according to the riches of His glory, to be strengthened with power through His Spirit in the inner man, so that Christ may dwell in your hearts through faith; and that you, being rooted and grounded in love, may be able to comprehend with all the saints what is the breadth and length and height and depth, and to know the love of Christ which surpasses knowledge, that you may be filled up to all the fullness of God.

Colossians 1:8-12

And who also told us of your love in the Spirit. For this reason, since the day we heard about you, we have not stopped praying for you. We continually ask God to fill you with the knowledge of his will through all the wisdom and understanding that the Spirit gives, so that you may live a life worthy of the Lord and please him in every way: bearing fruit in every good work, growing in the knowledge of God, being strengthened with all power according to his glorious might so that you may have great endurance and patience, and giving joyful thanks to the Father, who has qualified you to share in the inheritance of his holy people in the kingdom of light.

What is clear from theses and other similar passages from the Bible is that there is a definite link between wisdom and revelation and prayer. Wise people pray, and prayer opens the heavens for us to receive additional wisdom and revelation from on high. Connecting with Him who is All Wise had endless rewards.

A Spiritual Exercise

Insert the name of your loved one in the blanks below, and read this over them as you mediate on God's Word for the day.

Father God,

We pray right now for our loved ones according to the promise of Ephesians 1:15-23, ESV:

For this reason, because I have heard of [their] faith in the Lord Jesus, which exists among _____ and [their] love for all the saints, I do not cease giving thanks for _____ remembering _____ in my prayers; that the God of our Lord Jesus Christ, the Father of glory, may give to _____ the spirit of wisdom and of revelation in the knowledge of Him, having the eyes of _____'s heart enlightened, that _____ may know what is the hope to which [he/she] has been called _____, what are the riches of [his/her] glorious inheritance in the saints, and what is the immeasurable greatness of his power toward us who believe, according to the working of his great might that he worked in Christ when he raised him from the dead and seated him at his right hand in the heavenly places, far above all rule and authority and power and dominion, and above every name that is named, not only in this age but also in the one to come. And he put all things under his feet, and gave him as head over all things to the church, which is his body, the fullness of him who fills all in all.

NOTES

Faith

For we live by faith, not by sight.
2 Corinthians 5:7

Father,

Today I stand on Your faith, a faith that I may not see or feel. Faith means to have confidence. Lord, I have confidence that You are here and You are speaking to my heart about my situation. That situation weighs heavily upon my heart. I don't know how You are going to fix this, and I don't see the end to this road. But somehow I will lean on You and Your Word, which tells me to live by faith, and I will prevail.

I rest in the fact that this means I can take one step at a time. Just to move toward You is enough faith for You to fix this problem and turn it around. I may not see how You're going to turn it around. But You are working it out.

Thank You for sending Your angels that are helping me and moving on my behalf.

In Jesus' name,
Amen!

Faith

And now these three remain: faith, hope and love.
But the greatest of these is love.
1 Corinthians 13:13

Father,

Thank You for the gift of faith. Help me to use this gift today in my prayer life. Even through the most difficult times, Lord, stir up this gift in me. I pray for the kind of faith that would move obstacles out of my life and the life of my family members. I pray that You would help me to have faith, hope and love and to wear them as a necklace around my prayer life.

Let faith rise inside of me, faith to believe for the impossible. May I reach my hand of faith out to the hurting, those who are sick in body and sick in their heart. May I reach out to the world around me, and may the love of God be in my heart. Help me to move my selfish heart out of the way, so I can be more like Jesus. Let me love like Jesus and live like Jesus.

In Jesus' name,
Amen!

Faith

Be on your guard; stand firm in the faith;
be courageous; be strong.
1 Corinthians 16:13

Father,

I want to stand guard on the wall of prayer. Use me now to stand firm in my faith, as I walk with You and You guide me. In doing so, I will grow strong in my inner man.

Help me to be a constant and consistent person (with behavior, or process, unchanging in achievement or effect over a period) who has an effective prayer life, so that I will not grow weary in doing good.

I thank You now for keeping my eyes focused on You and not on any problem. Help me to be courageous and strong and walk in the fruit of love, so that love will overflow from my life. Give me inner strength, Lord, the kind of strength that can make me to stand during every battle. Give me the assurance that You are with me, speaking to my heart.

In Jesus' name,
Amen!

Faith

For it is by grace you have been saved, through faith —
and this is not from yourselves, it is the gift of God.
Ephesians 2:8

Father,

Wow! Thank You for such a wonderful and marvelous gift, the gift of grace (unmerited divine assistance). God, help me through even the most difficult times, when things seem unfair, slow, dead, fearful and the darkness may be all around me. I need Your salvation today. Come into my heart. Wash it clean. Give me new life and new hope for the future. Help me to press through the trials of life, so that I won't give up in the middle of the race. Call me to come up to another level, so that I can see things as they really are, not as my emotions might view them, but through Your gift, this gift called grace.

Show me what You did for me on the cross of Calvary so that I can fully accept the benefits of the free gift of salvation. There is so much more that You want for me and have for me.

In Jesus' name,
Amen!

The Prophetic and Prayer

Even on my servants, both men and women,
    I will pour out my Spirit in those days,
    and they will prophesy.   Acts 2:18

For some reason, the prophetic is a bazaar and scary topic for many today. In many churches, the prophetic is swept aside simply because people are afraid of it. When someone is gifted prophetically, too many consider them to be a super-spiritual hocus-pocus type of person. When God gave me this gift, I felt strange, out of place, and different, and really didn't know what to do or how to do it. It didn't help that the gift was frowned upon in many places.

Prophecy is not the same thing as preaching, as some have believed. The words preach and prophesy come from two entirely different Greek words. To preach means "to proclaim, announce, cry, or tell." Jesus said:

Go ye into all the world, and PREACH the gospel.   Mark 16:15, KJV
                                                        Emphasis Mine

Note that He did not say to prophesy the Gospel but to preach the Gospel.

The word *prophesy* means "to bubble up, to flow forth, or to cause to drop like rain." Teaching and preaching are preplanned, but prophecy is not. The Bible tells us that we are to *"despise not prophesyings. Prove all things"* (1 Thessalonians 5:20-21, KJV). When a prophecy is given, we are to test it and hold on to what is good in it.

When God first gave me this gift of prophecy, many pastors didn't welcome the prophetic as they do now. Often, they would ignore the gift and hope it would just go away. Today God has called His prophets to stand up like never before, and therefore pastors are more open to allowing prophetic activity in their services.

What exactly is the prophetic? And what does it have to do with prayer? I believe that the two go hand in hand and can be used as a weapon, a mighty force to tear down the kingdom of darkness.

Intercession is the training ground for the prophetic. Thus, the prophetic unction is received through prayer. Often I will feel the unction to pray in the Holy Spirit. Then comes a bubbling up, and after I have prayed in the Holy Spirit for a few minutes, I will feel a release, and God will use me to prophesy.

It doesn't always happen that same way. Sometimes, when I pray before a meeting, I will feel an unction to pray in the Holy Spirit, and sometimes that prayer will birth the prophetic to move in a meeting. I have to say that I am still learning how to move with the Holy Spirit in this gift.

In the context of this book on prayer, I can only touch the surface of this topic, but all I can say is that I do my best to follow the Holy Spirit, letting go of self and watching God move. I was blessed to sit under a pastor, a mighty man of God, who would flow in the gifts of the Spirit quite often and would never stop the flow in others. I learned a lot from him. He would often say, "It's the anointing that teaches us these things, and they are better caught not taught." So, always remember that the Holy Spirit is the best Teacher, and He will never lead you astray. Just follow His leading.

Also, remember to always test prophecy by the written Word of God. We can all miss God and sometimes prophesy in the flesh, but do not let that discourage you, and don't be swayed by what others say. Just seek more of God and read more of His Word. Follow the greatest Teacher in the world, the Holy Spirit. What a wonderful Teacher He is! His leading is always followed by peace.

Do not let a man hurry you to prophesy, but wait for the urging of the Spirit. Wait for Him to come before you attempt to speak. What a wonderful thing when God is holding your hand, leading His beloved to help His Church with this gift.

This brings me to a passage in the book of John, which reads as follows:

John 3:5-8

Jesus answered, "Very truly I tell you, no one can enter the kingdom of God unless they are born of water and the Spirit. Flesh gives birth to flesh, but the Spirit gives birth to spirit. You should not be surprised at my saying, 'You must be born again.' The wind blows wherever it pleases. You hear its sound, but you cannot tell where it comes from or where it is going. So it is with everyone born of the Spirit."

What does this have to do with prophecy and prayer? First, you cannot prophesy out of flesh, and neither can you pray out of the flesh. How do we know that some are doing this? The Scriptures admonish us:

1 Corinthian 14:1 and 4, ESV

Pursue love, and earnestly [If you do something earnestly, you do it in a serious, heartfelt way] *desire the spiritual gifts, especially that you may prophesy.*
The one who speaks in a tongue builds up himself, but the one who prophesies builds up the church.

This tells me that God wants us to have love for others, so love should be our highest goal, not to seek spiritual power for our own gain but to have true love for others.

It is clear that prophecy is not to be prohibited. Prophecy strengthens, encourages and comforts God's people (see 1 Corinthian 14:3). Prophecy has these components:

- Love
- Strength
- Encouragement
- Help
- Comfort

If you prophesy that someone will be losing their job or they will lose their house, that would not be very encouraging, so that would not be from God. If, on the other hand, you have a word that God is going to restore a family's finances, that would be encouraging and, thus, from God. Prophecy is "an inspired and anointed utterance, a supernatural proclamation in a known language." It is "a manifestation of the Spirit of God, not of our intellect" (see 1 Corinthians 12:7). This gift may be possessed and operated by all who have the infilling of the Holy Spirit (see 1 Corinthians 14:31).

There have been many prophecies over my own life, but I have tried to be careful not to move too quickly on prophecy or to believe every word of it. It is clear that we are to test anything and everything that is prophesied to us. Every word of it should be weighed against the Word of God.

1 John 5:7-9

For there are three that testify: the Spirit, the water and the blood; and the three are in agreement. We accept human testimony, but God's testimony is greater.

First John is telling us that everything that is in prophesied should point to God and never lift us (or some other person) up.

A family member prophesied to me concerning my marriage, that God was bringing a man into my life, someone who would love me and love my family, and together we would go into ministry. The prophecy said that it was "right around the corner." It didn't happen the next week, but about six months later, I met the man who became my husband.

Personally, I would be very careful about prophesying marriage over someone's life. In fact, I seldom see people use the gift of prophecy in that way. But God wanted me to be encouraged because my previous marriage had not been a happy one in any sense of the word. That marriage was filled with the world and all it had to offer. God was changing my life and restoring what the devil had stolen from me. It took seven years, but I waited patiently, and God gave me a husband who loves Him and loves me and is, in fact, a pastor.

I can always tell when the Spirit of prophecy comes into a room. The atmosphere shifts, and a Spirit of expectancy is felt. God knows when His people need encouragement, especially before or after a battle. Sometimes He will use me with the gift of prophecy or the gift of interpretation of tongues. This is the second of three inspirational or vocal gifts of the Holy Spirit. When combined with the inspirational gift of diverse tongues, the miraculous and supernatural phenomenon known as prophecy comes forth.

The Word of God teaches that if you speak in tongues, you should also pray that you will interpret those tongues. This is not only for the benefit of others, but for your own benefit as well. If someone speaks in tongues, you can ask God to move through you to give the interpretation so that others will understand, but you can also do this in your private prayers for your own personal benefit. You can pray, "Father, help me to understand what I've just said to You in the Spirit," and the Lord will give you the interpretation.

The Gifts of the Spirit and Prayer

1 Corinthians 12:1

Now about the gifts of the Spirit, brothers and sisters, I do not want you to be uninformed.

With these important words, Paul opened his teachings to the Corinthian believers concerning the gifts of the Spirit. The entire passage is worth reviewing:

1 Corinthians 12:1-11

Now about the gifts of the Spirit, brothers and sisters, I do not want you to be uninformed. You know that when you were pagans, somehow or other you were influenced and led astray to mute idols. Therefore I want you to know that no one who is speaking by the Spirit of God says, "Jesus be cursed," and no one can say, "Jesus is Lord," except by the Holy Spirit.

There are different kinds of gifts, but the same Spirit distributes them. There are different kinds of service, but the same Lord. There are different kinds of working, but in all of them and in everyone it is the same God at work.

Now to each one the manifestation of the Spirit is given for the common good. To one there is given through the Spirit a message of wisdom, to another a message of knowledge by means of the same Spirit, to another faith by the same Spirit, to another gifts of healing by that one Spirit, to another miraculous powers, to another prophecy, to another distinguishing between spirits, to another speaking in different kinds of tongues, and to still another the interpretation of tongues. All these are the work of one and the same Spirit, and he distributes them to each one, just as he determines.

There are nine spiritual gifts. They are:

- **The Gift of the Word of Wisdom**. This is a revelation gift (see 1 Corinthians 12:8). It is for the revealing of the prophetic future. It is speaking hidden truths of what is not yet known. It gives a supernatural perspective to ascertain the divine means for accomplishing God's will in a given situation. It is the divinely-given power to appropriate spiritual intuition in problem solving, a sense of divine direction, being led by the Holy Spirit to act appropriately in each set of circumstances, knowledge rightly applied.

- **The Gift of the Word of Knowledge**. This, again, is a revelation gift. It is the transcendental revelation of the divine will and plan of God and involves moral wisdom for right living and relationships, requires objective understanding concerning divine things in human duties, and refers to the knowledge of God or of the things that belong to God. As related in the Gospel, it is a supernatural revelation of the divine will and plan, supernatural insights. It implies a deeper and more advanced understanding of the communicated acts of God and involves moral wisdom for right living. It is related to Good News.

- **The Gift of Discerning of Spirits**. Another of the revelation gifts (see 1 Corinthians 12:10), this gift allows the believer to clearly distinguish truth from error by judging whether the behavior or teaching is from God, Satan or man. It is a supernatural power to detect the realm of the spirits and their activity and implies the power of spiritual insight and supernatural revelations of the plans and purposes of the enemy and his forces.

- **The Gift of Faith**. This is one of the power gifts (see 1 Corinthians 12:8-10) which allows a Spirit-filled believer to be firmly persuaded of God's power and promises to accomplish His will and purpose and to display such a confidence in Him and His Word that circumstances and obstacles do not shake that conviction. It is the supernatural ability to believe God without doubting, the supernatural ability to combat unbelief, an inner conviction impelled by an urgent and higher calling.

- **The Gifts of Healing.** This is another of the power gifts (see 1 Corinthians 12:9) to be used as a means through which God makes people whole physically, emotionally, mentally or spiritually. It is supernatural healing without human aid and includes divine assistance. The gifts of healing do not doubt God's power.

- **The Gift of Miracles.** This is another of the power gifts (see 1 Corinthians 12:10). When the gift of miracles is in operation, a believer is enabled by God to perform mighty deeds which witnesses acknowledge to be of supernatural origin and means. This gift bypasses the natural and operates in conjunction with the gift of faith for healing the sick and taking authority over sin and Satan.

- **The Gift of Prophecy.** This is one of the vocal gifts (see 1 Corinthians 12:10). The gift of prophecy edifies, exhorts and comforts. It helps build us up or strengthen us and should lead us to the Word of God. It is the ministry of the Holy Spirit to convict of sin, of righteousness and of judgment to come (see John 16:8-11). It may also manifest in the form of dance, worship or art, and is often used in conjunction with other gifts. It may be used for declaring the will of God for a nation or for an individual.

- **The Gift of Divers Kinds of Tongues.** Another of the vocal gifts, this is a supernatural utterance given through a believer. By the power of the Holy Spirit, they will speak something in a language they have never learned. The Holy Spirit energizes their tongue to edify believers through language and music. It conveys spiritual insight into the plans of God and edifies the Body of Christ.

- **The Gift of Interpretation of Tongues.** Another vocal gift, this one is a supernatural verbalization, an interpretation that reveals the meaning of a message in tongues. It operates out of the mind of the Spirit rather than out of the mind of man and functions in the Spirit, not in the mind, will or emotions. It is used by the God to interpret a message given through the gift of tongues so that all will understand what God is saying.

God will often use these gifts through the ministers appointed to care for His flock. These can be found in Ephesians 4:11, where it states that they are given by

Christ Himself. They are apostles, prophets, evangelists, pastors and teachers. Define each of the following titles and descriptions:

Apostles:

Prophets:

Evangelists:

Pastors/Teachers:

Missionaries:

Special Graces:

Hospitality:

Celibacy:

Martyrdom:

Wisdom as It Relates to the Gifts of the Spirit

Some people have a special ministry in one of the nine gifts, for example, wisdom. If we need an answer and direction about a certain situation, God will use the gift of wisdom and/or other spiritual gifts to supply it. There are three types of wisdom:

- The wisdom of God (see 1 Corinthians 2:6-7)
- The wisdom of the world (see 1 Corinthians 2:6)
- The wisdom of man (see Ecclesiastes 1:16-18)

The gift of the word of wisdom is the application of knowledge that God gives you to perceive correctly (see 1 Corinthians 2:6-7). This type of wisdom is a gift which cannot be gained through study or experience and should by no means try to replace them. The gift of the word of wisdom is seeing life from God's perspective. As a Christian exercises this gift, he or she begins to develop a fear of the Lord. This is *"the beginning of wisdom,"* according to Proverbs 1:7.

The gift of the word of wisdom is also the revealing of prophetic future. It is speaking hidden truths of what is not yet known. It is a supernatural perspective to ascertain the divine means for accomplishing God's will in each situation and is a divinely given power to appropriate spiritual intuition in problem solving. Furthermore, this gift involves having a sense of divine direction, being led by the Holy Spirit to act appropriately in each set of circumstances, and rightly applying knowledge.

The gift of wisdom is the wisdom of God. It is the supernatural impartation of facts. It is not natural in any sense of the word. You cannot earn it. It is received from God through prayer (see Ephesians 1:17). This gift, the word of wisdom, works interactively with the other two revelation gifts: knowledge and discernment.

All gifts are given by the Spirit of God and are given to encourage, edify and build up, so that the Church can go forth in the things God and work for His purpose and His will. God delights in us being involved with His work. He is so gracious that by His Holy Spirit He freely distributes spiritual gifts to all who desire them. He not only wants us to know our spiritual gifts, but He expects us to grow in them each day.

Knowing the Giver of All Gifts Better

Rather than concentrate on receiving certain gifts, we must concentrate on developing our personal relationship with the Giver of All Gifts, and that is done through prayer. That He is the Giver cannot be in question. He has said:

Therefore I want you to know that no one who is speaking by the Spirit of God says, "Jesus be cursed," and no one can say, "Jesus is Lord," except by the Holy Spirit. There are different kinds of gifts, but the same Spirit distributes them. There are different kinds of service, but the same Lord. There are different kinds of working, but in all of them and in everyone it is the same God at work.
1 Corinthians 12:3–6, ESV

It is the one and only Spirit Who Distributes all these gifts and he alone decides which gift each person should have. 1 Corinthians 12:11, NLT

Now we have received not the spirit of the world, but the Spirit who is from God, that we might understand the things freely given us by God. And we impart this in words not taught by human wisdom but taught by the Spirit, interpreting spiritual truths to those who are spiritual. 1 Corinthians 2:12–13, ESV

I was praying as I wrote this book and I asked God to help me to prophesy in it. Instead, He told me to give an example of the gift and how He uses it through me. Many times, when I prophesy (which is the strongest gift in my life, along with intercession), His Spirit will come upon me. I will wait for a person to stop speaking in tongues, and then I will pray in the Holy Spirit, and God will give me the interpretation of that message in tongues. This leads me to prophesy. That's one of the ways God uses me.

I have seen others just start prophesying over a person, as the Spirit leads them. Remember to always wait for the Holy Spirit to move upon you before you prophesy. Never prophe-lie! Also remember that you are speaking into the life of another human being, someone God cares about deeply. At that particular moment, they may need your word more than you can realize.

God is gentle (He's a gentleman), and He never rushes into anything. He never pushes Himself upon anybody. Just wait for His gentle urge for you to speak. God's Word says that He is peace, so wait for His peace to come. In the beginning, it may feel as if you cannot contain yourself, for the fire burns so brightly in your heart. That may indicate that the gift is starting to manifest.

When God gave me this gift, for the next couple of years I prophesied to everyone I met, but that was because God was taking so much out of me. His anointing was coming in to fill the places where He had taken bad stuff out. Some people were upset by my exuberance, but I just prophesied and let God teach me through the experience. I was so hungry that I didn't care what anyone thought or said.

As I noted before, when God gave me this gift, it seemed that people were afraid of it. Now everyone seems to be prophesying. This gift is being used by God more than ever before, and everyone seems to desire it.

Recently, I was talking to a pastor friend of mine, and she was telling me that she now has classes to teach people how to stir up this gift within them. How wonderful to know that God is using her to help others reach their spiritual goals in life! My own pastor would always encourage me to prophesy in the church. At first, my self-esteem was so beat up from the past, and I believe God used this gift to give me back my self-esteem. He showed me who I was in Him. I was so hungry to learn more about this gift that I would study for hours at a time. The gift of prophecy is such a wonderful gift. It can bring people to salvation and help them be filled them with the Holy Ghost right then and there.

But, again, prayer is essential. How can we speak for God if we cannot hear and know His voice?

The Fruit of the Spirit and Prayer

But the fruit of the Spirit is love, joy, peace, forbearance, kindness, goodness, faithfulness, gentleness and self-control. Against such things there is no law.

Galatians 5:22-23

Now that we have discussed the gifts of the Spirit, we must also discuss the fruit of the Spirit. Without the fruit of the Spirit in our lives, we can easily fall into error and actually begin to use the spiritual gifts for fleshly reasons and not wait for and carefully obey the Holy Spirit.

We must seek the fruit of patience. This fruit will bring order to our lives. No one likes this particular fruit, but it is vital to help us to grow spiritually. Without the fruit of the Spirit, we might even lash out at others in anger, resentment, bitterness or jealous, and God certainly doesn't want us to hurt each other. In fact, He severely warned us against it:

But whoso shall offend one of these little ones which believe in me, it were better for him that a millstone were hanged about his neck, and that he were drowned in the depth of the sea.   Matthew 18:6, KJV

God loves His little ones, and we should too. Therefore He begins this work in us called "the fruit of the Spirit."

The Holy Spirit is working these fruits into us to help us gain character. These fruits of the Spirit are just the opposite of the fruits of the flesh. Jesus taught:

75

Even so, every good tree bears good fruit, but a bad tree bears bad fruit. A good tree cannot bear bad fruit, nor can a bad tree bear good fruit. Every tree that does not bear good fruit is cut down and thrown into the fire. Therefore by their fruits you will know them.   Matthew 7:17-20, NKJV

This passage helps us to understand the behaviors of people who have allowed the grace of the Holy Spirit to be active in their lives. *Love, joy, peace, forbearance, kindness, goodness, faithfulness, gentleness and self-control* ... this is the life in the Spirit. It is acquired through prayer, through an intimate relationship with the Father of Righteousness.

Music and Prayer

But those who wait on the LORD
Shall renew their strength;
They shall mount up with wings like eagles,
They shall run and not be weary,
They shall walk and not faint.   Isaiah 40:31, NKJV

Music and quietness have always been essential to our times of communion with God, and the Bible is filled with music and with times of waiting in His presence. Too often and too soon the music is suspended before the Holy Spirit is able to move in a special way. There are times when Holy Spirit wants to move in our midst, but we are in such a hurry to leave or to do something else that He cannot do it. If we will just wait on Him, quieting our souls, we can hear the angels moving around. If we can just stay silent long enough to listen, it is amazing what God will say to us. In our quietness, we can sense the "wind," "breath" or "Spirit" of God (*ruach* in Hebrew), moving about. If you are weary or heavy laden, today would be good time to refresh your soul with a time of worship. Oh, how sweet it is to wait upon the Lord while listening to good worship music or, better yet, while personally singing His praises!

When I minister, there are times when I can hear the Lord saying, "Child, just be still." If I obey, He comes in like a wind and does wonders in our midst.

Again, the Holy Spirit is a gentleman. He will not shove His way through the door of our hearts. He will not push His way through our life. In the same way, He will not push His way through a song service. When He is welcomed, He will come as a wind and just hover over and around us, waiting for us to acknowledge who He is by lifting Him up with our music. I have been in many dry churches where people just hurried through a song service so that they could go get something to eat. What a waste of time that is! How can we succumb to religion? That doesn't do anything for your soul. It leaves you dry and cold. When it's over, the people leave exactly as they came. They are not changed. If we could just wait for the Holy Spirit to move through our music, people would leave full, changed and refreshed. When that happens, we know that God has breathed upon us.

It was that breath that made us living creatures, or living beings, way back in the beginning:

Genesis 2:7, NIV

Then the LORD God formed a man from the dust of the ground and breathed into his nostrils the breath of life, and the man became a living being.

This *ruach* is the breath of both animals and mankind, and it is the very breath of God's nostrils. As God breathed into us, life came in. He is the Creator, and His breath brings life. Just as it was in the beginning, we still need the breath of God today to keep our spirits alive and well, and one of the most common ways we experience the breath of God is through anointed music.

I love good worship music, I love to worship the Lord, and I often begin to feel His presence with me in a special way through music. When there is anointed music and when I can enter in and worship the Lord, that's when I can minister more effectively. The most anointed music comes to us through a prophetic musical gifting. When this happens, a birthing of a fresh word comes forth. My spirit is ignited and the prophetic gifts manifest.

That's how we can know that the Holy Spirit has been in a service. We look back and remember how good it was and how glad we were to be in the House of the Lord and experience His Shekinah glory. I would not trade such times for anything. For days afterward, we have such joy.

Today, I trust that you can find a private place in your home or under the shade of a nice tree. Relax, kick off your shoes, and wait for the Holy Spirit to come. Yes, He is there, close by your side. Quiet your soul, and let Him speak to the depths of your being. Find that place of intimacy today.

A Prayer for Family

For if you remain silent now,
relief and deliverance will arise for the Jews from another place
but you and your father's family will perish.
And who knows but that you have come to your royal position
for such a time as this?
Esther 4:14

Father,

Use me in this time of prayer to help my family and bring deliverance to them. Have grace and mercy on my family. Help me to be a light to them and to show them Your love.

I humble myself before You and ask that You open their eyes so that they can see that they need You so desperately. Today I stand as a royal queen, decreeing Your word over their lives.

In Jesus' name,
Amen!

"In the silence of the heart God speaks. If you face God in prayer and supplication, God will speak to you Then you will know that you are nothing. It is only when you realize your nothingness, your emptiness, that God can fill you with Himself. Souls of prayer are souls of silence."

— Mother Teresa

A Prayer for Family

Look and see, for everyone is coming home!
your sons are coming from distant lands; your
little daughters will be carried home.
Isaiah 60:4, NLT

Father,

Draw our children to You. Cover them and hold them close.
Bring our children from distant lands, and bring us together in health and harmony.

In Jesus' name,
Amen

Write your own prayer here:!

A Prayer for Family

And it shall come to pass in the last days, saith God,
I will pour out of my Spirit upon all flesh;
and your sons and your daughters shall prophesy,
and your young men shall see visions,
and your old men shall dream dreams.
Acts 2:17, KJV

Father,

Thank You for pouring out Your Spirit on our family in these last days. May the Spirit of Revelation be poured out upon our children and young people. Move and stir up the gift of prophecy over our loved ones.

In Jesus' name,
Amen!

Write your own prayer here:

A Prayer for Family

We will not hide them from their children,
showing to the generation to come the praises of the LORD,
and his strength, and his wonderful
works that he hath done.
Psalm 78:4, KJV

Father,

We ask You, Do not hide Your truth from our children. Help us to tell the next generation about Your glorious deeds and Your power. Show our children Your wonderful kindness, and help them to stand for what is right, so that they may be a light to their generation.

In Jesus' name,
Amen

Write your own prayer here:!

A Prayer for Health

This was fulfilling what was spoken through the prophet Isaiah,
"He took up our infirmities
and bore our diseases."
Matthew 8:17

Holy Spirit,

We ask You to touch our bodies and to take away any pain that may be affecting us. Touch my inner parts and align everything back to the way it is supposed to be.

I know that it is Your plan that I am healed.

I pray for my family and friends today who are in the hospital and need a touch from You.

In Jesus' name,
Amen!

Write your own prayer here:

A Prayer for Health

Beloved, I wish above all things
that thou mayest prosper
and be in health,
even as thy soul prospereth.
3 John 1:2, KJV

Father,

I know that it is Your will that I be in good health and prosper. Today I stand on Your Word and speak it out of my mouth, believing in my heart for healing. If anybody in my family is in pain due to sickness, relieve their pain today and comfort them.

In Jesus' name,
Amen!

Write your own prayer here:

A Prayer for Provision

But thou shalt remember the LORD thy God:
for it is he that giveth thee power to get wealth,
that he may establish his covenant
which he sware unto thy fathers,
as it is this day.
Deuteronomy 8:18, KJV

Father,

Give us increase in our jobs, relationships and family. We follow Your commands, so that You may give us increase, and we may possess everything You have for us.

I will follow Your voice. Lead and guide me to those places I need to be.

In Jesus' name,
Amen!

Write your own prayer here:

A Prayer for Provision

Give, and it shall be given unto you; good measure,
pressed down, and shaken together, and running over,
shall men give into your bosom. For with the same measure
that ye mete withal it shall be measured to you again.
Luke 6:38, KJV

Father,

I give You today all of my money. May it be poured out to You as a sacrifice. Use what I give to help the homeless and the less fortunate. Forgive me for the times I did not heed Your voice to give more. When I am obedient, You said that in return You would give back to me in an overflow. Use my sacrifice to feed the needy and homeless and to bring provision for the House of God.

In Jesus' name,
Amen!

Write your own prayer here:

A Prayer for Miracles

By stretching forth thine hand to heal;
and that signs and wonders may be done
by the name of thy holy child Jesus.
Act 4:30, KJV

Father,

Use my hands to heal the sick by showing forth Your signs and wonders. I humble myself under Your authority and take hold of healing for myself, my friends and my family members. I ask that You stretch forth Your hand to heal.

In Jesus' name,
Amen!

Write your own prayer here:

A Prayer for Miracles

And God wrought special miracles by the hands of Paul;
so that from his body were brought unto the sick handkerchiefs or aprons,
and the diseases departed from them
and evil spirits went out of them.
Acts 19:11-12, KJV

Father,

We ask for Your special miracles today. Just as You used Paul with special miracles, I ask that You use me in that same way. Lord, I ask for Your miracle to manifest in my life. I know that doubt and unbelief has crept in and I should believe more for Your miraculous power. Forgive me for the time I doubted You. Now I know that You can and want to do miracles through me. So let all disease depart from my family, friends and loved ones.

In Jesus' name,
Amen!

Write your own prayer here:

Psalm 23 and Prayer

The LORD is my Shepard, I lack nothing
He makes me lie down in green pastures,
He leads me beside quiet waters,
He refreshes my soul.
He guides me along the right paths
For his name's sake
Even though I walk
Through the darkest valley
I will fear no evil,
For you are with me;
Your rod and your staff,
They comfort me.
Psalm 23:1-4

In Jesus' name,
Amen!

Father,

Hush the waters and lead my soul to rest, as You refresh and hold me in Your presence for Your name's sake. Though my valley may be dark, I will not fear, for You are with me. You give me hope in the midst of my storm.

Protect me in Your loving arms today. Guard my mind from the evil that would try to influence me with thoughts that are negative. Remind me, Lord, that I am Yours and You are mine. Help me to keep resting in You. I know, without a shadow of a doubt, that Your rod and staff comfort me and support me.

Thank You for being a shepherd who cares for me enough to protect me from the dangers of life, as they may come like foxes and bears. I cry out to You today, and I know You are listening.

In Jesus' name,
Amen!

"During times of struggle and danger, Jesus is always there to comfort us with His rod and staff. The meaning of the Hebrew words translated rod (*sebet*) and *staff* (*mishena*) are very special. The Hebrew word *sebet* has the idea of 'a stick.' It originally referred to a part of a tree. In the Old Testament, the stick was used to count sheep (see Leviticus 27:32). It was also used to protect the sheep from other animals.

In the book of Proverbs, the stick was used for discipline (see Proverbs 13:24). *Sebet* carries a sense of authority.

"The Hebrew word *mishena* conveys the idea of 'something to lean on, trust, support or staff.' Together, the two words paint a picture of a strong, protective shepherd whom we can trust, one who not only cares for us, but who also will protect us.

"Sheep are stupid animals compared to other creatures. If we are following the shepherd, and danger, trouble, and the threat of death come in the form of life's foxes and bears, He is there with His rod and staff. He protects us with His rod, and we can trust the leading of His staff. Do you feel like crying out, 'Baa, baa, baa?' He is listening!" [4]

---

4. https://www.neverthirsty.org/bible-qa/qa-archives/question/what-do-the-terms-rod-and-staff-mean-in-the-23rd-psalm/

A Prayer for Joy

You make known to me the path of life;
In your presence, there is fullness of joy;
At your right hand are pleasures forevermore.
Psalm 16:11, NKJV

Father,

Show me Your path of life for me and help me to escape from anything that would cause death in my life. I enter now into Your presence where there is fullness of joy and eternal life, given to me by the resurrected Savior, Jesus Christ, Whom I trust. I know that sometimes I want to do my own thing, but this does not bring forth the life-giving path You have for me. Sometimes I feel that my path is filled with doubt, unbelief and sickness, but that is not what You want for me. I know the path that You lead me to brings life, joy, goodness and satisfaction.

In Jesus' name,
Amen!

Write your own prayer here:

A Prayer for Joy

My brethren,
count it all joy when you fall into various trials,
knowing that the testing of your faith produces patience.
James 1:2, NKJV

Father,

Thank You for all my trials. Help me to know that each one may lead me to faith and give me joy to endure whatever You may place in my way. Give me faith to believe for my family and friends. I know that I will pass this test that produces patience.

In Jesus' name,
Amen!

Write your own prayer here:

A Prayer for Protection

Finally, be strong in the Lord and in his mighty power.
Put on the full armor of God.
Stand firm then, with the belt of truth buckled around your waist,
with the breastplate of righteousness in place,
and with your feet fitted
with the readiness that comes from the gospel of peace.
In addition to all this, take up the shield of faith,
with which you can extinguish all the flaming arrows of the evil one.
Ephesians 6:10 and 14-16

Dear God, today we put on the full armor to guard our lives against attack. We put on the belt of truth to protect against lies and deception. We put on the breastplate of righteousness to protect our hearts from the temptations we face. We put the Gospel of peace on our feet so we're ready to take Your light wherever You send us. We choose to walk in the peace and freedom of your Spirit and not be overcome with fear and anxious thoughts. We take up your shield of faith that will extinguish all the darts and threats hurled our way by the enemy. We believe in Your power to protect us and choose to trust in You. We put on the helmet of salvation, which covers our minds and thoughts, reminding us we are children of the day, forgiven, set free, saved by the grace of Christ Jesus. We take up the sword of the Spirit, your very Word, the one offensive weapon given to us for battle, which has the power to demolish strongholds. It is alive, active, and sharper than any double-edged sword.

We ask for Your help in remembering to put on Your full armor every day, for You give us all that we need to stand firm in this world. Forgive us, God, for the times we've been unprepared, too busy to care, or trying to fight and wrestle in our own strength.

In Jesus' name,
Amen!

A Prayer for Peace

Peace I leave with you;
my peace I give you.
I do not give to you as the world gives.
Do not let your hearts be troubled
and do not be afraid.
John 14:27

Father,

Give me peace now. I know that the peace You give is not like the false peace the world offers through things. You can settle my heart and keep me from being fearful because of the troubles of this world: bills, distractions and family problems. I rest in Your peace now, and I am still before You. Let Your peace comfort my heart like a blanket.

In Jesus' name,
Amen!

Write your own prayer here:

Peace lights the way to the path where I find
Rest in the Holy Spirit.
A gentle touch from
Angel wings from heaven to my heart.
— Author Unknown

In the middle of God's will is peace from within.
It settles in your heart,
and you know that you can be at rest.
— Author Unknown

But he was pierced for our transgressions,
he was crushed for our iniquities;
the punishment that brought us peace was on him,
and by his wounds we are healed.
Isaiah 53:5 [5]

---

[5]. Memorize this verse today

A Prayer for Peace

And may the Lord of peace Himself
give to you peace always and in every way.
2 Thessalonians 3:16, YLT

Father,

We thank You for the peace that will penetrate our mind. We know that You can slow our thoughts down and help us, Lord, with worry, fear, doubt and the troubles that bombard our heart and mind. You have given us this great promise to help us in every way through every situation. There is nothing You cannot do, but we just need to rest and wait on Your direction—even through the most difficult of times.

In Jesus' name,
Amen!

Write your own prayer here:

A Prayer for Revelation

Children, you belong to God,
and you have defeated these enemies.
God's Spirit is in you
and is more powerful
than the one that is in the world.
1 John 4:4, CEV

Father,

I am Your child, and I thank You that I have the victory over anything that might try to come against me. You said that the Spirit that lives in me is greater than anything that would come to hinder my life.

In Jesus name,
Amen!

Write your own prayer here:

A Prayer for Revelation

In the beginning was the Word, and the Word was
With God, and the Word was God.
John 1:1, KJV

Father,

Speak to me through Your Word, and let it come alive in my heart and soul. Speak to my family and friends through Your Word.

In Jesus' name,
Amen!

Write your own prayer here:

A Prayer for Miracles

For I am not ashamed of the gospel of Christ:
for it is the power of God unto salvation
to ever one that believeth;
to the Jew first, and also to the Greek.
Romans 1:16, KJV

Father,

I am not ashamed of the Gospel. Help me to be a witness for You. Help me to spread Your Word among the lost. Move with miracles signs and wonders for them that follow You. I pray for miracles now.

In Jesus' name,
Amen!

Write your own prayer here:

A Prayer for Love

Beloved, if God so loved us,
we ought also to love one another.
1 John 4:11, KJV

Father,

I love You, and I pray for Your love to shine through me today to those at my job and to my family and friends, so that You will be glorified. Help me to love even the unlovable, the rejected and the poor.

In Jesus' name,
Amen!

Write your own prayer here:

A Prayer of Repentance

Peter replied, "Repent and be baptized, every one of you,
in the name of Jesus Christ for the forgiveness of your sins.
And you will receive the gift of the Holy Spirit."
Acts 2:38

Father,

I repent for anything that I have done to cause You sadness. Please forgive any sins that I have committed. I receive Your gift of the Holy Spirit.

In Jesus' name,
Amen!

Write your own prayer here:

A Prayer for Holy Spirit Guidance

But you will receive power when the Holy Spirit comes on you;
and you will be my witnesses in Jerusalem, and in all Judea
and Samaria, and to the ends of the earth.
Acts 1:8

Father,

I want to be a good witness, Lord, in my home, on my job and all the other places I go. I ask for Your power to come upon me, so that I can speak Your Word boldly. Use me today and help me to become obedient to Your Word.

In Jesus' name,
Amen!

Write your own prayer here:

A Prayer of Repentance

If we confess our sins
[sin can be viewed as any thought or action that endangers
the ideal relationship between an individual and God],
he is faithful and just to forgive us our sins,
and purify us from all unrighteousness.
1 John 1:9

Father,

I come to You today and ask that You forgive me for any sins that I have committed that have endangered our relationship. I come back to You now, and ask that the sin that has caused You grief and caused me separation from You be forgiven. Forgive me from any greed, lust, sexual immorality, impurity and debauchery, idolatry and sorcery, hatred, discord, jealousy and rage, rivalries, divisions or factions. I know now that without a doubt our relationship is deeper than ever. Catch me while I fall into Your loving arms.

In Jesus' name,
Amen!

Write your own prayer here:

A Prayer for Salvation

Everyone who calls on the name of the Lord
will be saved.
Romans 10:13, NLT

Heavenly Father,

I admit that I am a sinner in need of a Savior. Forgive me of my sins. You said that You had come to save that which was lost:

For the Son of man is come to seek and to save that which was lost.
Luke 19:10, NIV

I am lost without You. I believe in my heart that You died and rose again. Come into my heart. I call upon You now. Come, Holy Spirit, wash me clean.

In Jesus name,
Amen!

Peace and Prayer

I pray that God, the source of hope, will fill you completely with joy and peace because you trust in him. Then you will overflow with confident hope through the power of the Holy Spirit.   Romans 15:13, NLT

"The petition in this verses is that God would fill with 'peace,' with a sense of their peace with him, made by the blood of Christ, with a conscience peace in their own breasts, arising from a view of their justification by the righteousness of Christ, and from the sprinklings of His blood upon them, and also with peace one among another, unspeakable, and full of glory. Peace comes in at the door of faith. There is no true peace until a soul is brought to believe in Christ, and that is promoted and increased by repeated acts of faith in Christ or by a constant living by faith in Him."[6]

How wonderful it is to know that God, the Lord of the Universe, would be so kind as to fill our hearts with the one thing we need the most—peace, wonderful peace! Oh, beloved, I hope that through this prayer guide you have been able to see that God wants to give us peace in our lives. Through your hurt, pain, offenses, unforgiveness and fear, He wants to give you the one thing that can help you through life's hurdles—peace, peace, wonderful peace! It can be found in His presence and we enter His presence through prayer.

You know that He is the Prince of Peace, so grab hold of this fact today. Then, when bill collectors call, your children are screaming and life is putting other demands on you, hold on to His peace. Learn to hold on to it even in your worst times of hurt and distress.

6. *Gill's Exposition of the Entire Bible* from www.biblehub.com

So many times I have felt that I was on the brink of my fears toppling over on me and crushing me. But then, God, in His great love, came and filled my heart with His peace. There are days when I can feel the room filled with so much peace. Everything around me seems to be illuminated by God's presence and His peace. My prayer is that today, right now, you, too, can experience that presence and that peace in prayer.

When you have done everything you know to do, remember: God is in charge, and everything He gives us is good. Just stand in His presence, sit in His presence, kneel in His presence or lie in His presence and bask in His peace. After all, He is the God of peace:

And the peace of God, which passeth all understanding, shall keep your hearts and minds through Christ Jesus. Philippians 4:7, KJV

If you could just know how loved you are today and how valuable you are to God, I'm certain that it would change everything for you. Just look around you. See the trees, the flowers, the birds. He has created it all just for you because He loves you so much. Experience His presence today. He will not hide from you.

Believe me He is right there beside you even now, looking lovingly at you, awaiting your response. He will not reject you, no matter what you have done, even if you have rejected Him or if you failed Him today. In the time of your greatest misery, He is there. In your most broken times, He is there.

Yes! You are His, and He is yours! If everyone else rejected you or forsook you, He still would not. He would stick very close to you and help you rebuild what was lost. Oh, beloved, He has done it for me, and I know He will do it for you too.

There is nothing you can do to earn God's love. He loves you because He created you in the first place, and He did it with purpose. He loves you just the way you are, and He will love you always!

Experiencing God's presence is so easy. He's there with you now! I leave you with this last Bible promise (the most important of all).

Romans 10:13

Everyone who calls on the name of the Lord will be saved.

The greatest thing you could ever experience is to know God and have the blessing of His presence with you. Accept Him today into your heart as Lord and Savior. Once you have begun this journey, you will never ever want to leave it! God's presence will be forever engraved on the tables of your heart. Invite Him in today, and He will never leave you! Then enjoy your privileged relationship with Him every single moment of every single day. As one of the shortest verses in the Bible says:

Pray without ceasing.   1 Thessalonians 5:17

                                                                          Amen!

Author Contact Page

You may contact Debby Gautreaux in the following way:

belovedroses3@aol.com